Low Carb

40 Great Weight Loss Recipes For Griddle Or Slow Cooker With Almost Zero Carbs

Table of content

HIGH FAT LOW CARB

GRIDDLE RECIPES

TOP 20 SIMPLE & HEALTHY GRIDDLER RECIPES FOR RAPID WEIGHT LOSS

IMOGEN BUSH

Low Carb Cookbook.

20 Griddler Low Carb Recipes For Weight Watchers

Easy Griddle Cooking.

Introduction

Thank you for buying this book! The panini press griddler is a fantastic way to cook some of your favorites. It's quick, it's easy, and it's versatile. You should know that it's used for more than just making a delicious panini. However, when you buy one, you may think that you can only grill burgers and chicken on there. While those taste great, there's plenty of other recipes out there, and they'll make your mouth water. These treats are easy to make and are quite delicious! From breakfast, lunch, dinner, and dessert, this book will cover all meals, with five recipes for each of them.

Note that you don't necessarily have to have a Panini Press to cook these. Any indoor grill will work. For best results, however, a Panini Press is recommended. If you have a Foreman, it'll work too.

Chapter 1 – The Grilling Revolution

A long time ago, it used to be quite cumbersome to grill something. You had to set up a bulky grill, grab the coal, and light a fire. If weather conditions weren't ideal, there was no grilling for you. Indoor grills did exist, but they were for fancy restaurants.

But those times have changed. While nothing beats a hamburger over a flame, indoor grilling comes close. Indoor grills are relatively inexpensive and allow anyone to cook delicious recipes in no time at all. There are many indoor grills out there. Some lock in all the flavor, and some drain the fat for a healthier meal. There are panini presses out there that will give you a great panini, a grilled sandwich that doesn't use sliced bread. Once you have an indoor grill, you practically never have to eat out again.

However, many people undervalue their grills. They think that you can make a few sandwiches or meats, and that's it. But that's not the case! You can make a good meal using your grill. In the next few chapters, you'll learn about just a few of the recipes that you can cook with your panini press. These recipes don't necessarily require that, but it is recommended. All grills are made different, so check to see if your grill's surface is adjustable, if it has heat settings, or if it has a drip tray.

A few other tips are as follows:

1. Always preheat the grill before you cook. This should be common sense, but many people forget that. You want to expose the food to the temperature that it needs to cook all the time when it's cooking, so if it's less, it may be overcooked.

2. All griddles aren't created equal. Some may give off different temperatures than others. Some grills only have one set temperature. Some use numbers instead of words. Because of this, make sure to check your food when it's in the range of the recommended minutes. It may need more time, or it may need less. Do not mess it up by overcooking or undercooking your meal.

3. Make sure to check to see if your griddle is nonstick or not. If it's not, you need to grease up your grills so it doesn't stick. Use some fat-free cooking spray for best results.

4. Make sure to check the thickness of what you're grilling. If it's too thick, it may take longer to cook. If one food is thicker than the other, the grill may close its lid on one and not the other, cooking them unequally. Measure beforehand so you don't face the consequences.

5. Always clean after every use. This means that you should invest in a scraper so you can scrape your grill beforehand. Empty your drip tray on occasion too. If your grills are removable, you can use your dishwasher or sink for easy cleaning. Don't put it in the water if the grill is attached, however. Water may damage your unit.

6. Adjust your grill accordingly. Some recipes may require your grill to be flat, others tilted. See if your grill is adjustable beforehand.

7. Finally, have fun with what you cook. Remember that cooking can be about experimentation as well. Because of this, you may want to try some of your own recipes. Feel free to modify the provided recipes as well, and adjust to your liking. If you're a vegetarian or vegan, substitute the meats and dairy products. If you don't like a food, such as onions, take it out or replace it with something you do like. This book is merely a way get you started, and the recipes aren't the end-all, be all. Adjust the amount of ingredients to your liking, and experiment.

Chapter 2 – A Grilled Breakfast

Breakfast is the most important meal of the day, and everyone strives for a hearty meal that will help them break the fast. But not everyone has the time to cook a great meal every day. Some may fix something quick, or nothing at all. However, you need a good meal if you want to survive the world, and because of this, you should make sure you're getting enough food. Indoor grilling can help with that.

There are plenty of breakfast dishes you can fix with your panini press or indoor grill, and they'll give you diner-quality meals for cheap and in no time at all. These recipes are quick and easy to make.

Bacon

The traditional way of cooking bacon is through the pan. However, you can get the same crispy results through a panini press. No having to worry about grease popping, either.

What You Need

- Six slices of raw bacon

Directions

1. Preheat the press to around medium-high, installing the drip pan if it has one. If it can tilt, make sure to do that first.

2. Place the bacon slices in a neat fashion, making sure they don't overlap. You may need to trim the bacon if your press is small.

3. After that, simply close the lid and wait for about 10-14 minutes.

4. If you have a grill where you can change the upper plate's height, adjust so that it barely touches the top of the bacon, for best results. Depending on the thickness it may take more time.

5. Remove the strips once cooked and enjoy!

Delicious Hashbrowns

What You Need

- 30 oz of shredded potatoes, frozen.
- 1/3 cup of olice oil
- 1 tsp salt. Adjust to taste.
- ½ tsp of paprika
- ¼ tsp of black pepper
- Feel free to add cheese, jalapeños, diced ham, or anything else to the mix as well.

Directions

1. Set your press to medium-high heat.

2. Combine all ingredients in a large bowl, tossing as you do in order to combine.

3. Once the press is heated, spoon your mix on your press and close the lid tightly.

4. Cook for 5-10 minutes, depending on how crispy you like your hashbrowns. Remove from the press and add more mixture.

Health Omelet

If you want something filling in under 400 calories, this omelet will do it. At just 350 calories, it packs quite a punch of flavor.

What You Need

- ¼ cup of egg product, i.e. Egg Beaters
- ¼ cup diced onion
- 1 diced jalapeno
- 1 tbsp diced Roma tomato
- 1 tbsp of reduced fat cheese, preferably Mexican
- 1 diced red potato, about the size of a golf ball
- 2 sausage links
- Salt and pepper for taste
- Any kind of tobasco sauce to taste, optional
- Cooking spray

Directions

1. Heat your press to high. Spray it with the cooking spray. Dice your potato in even slices. Then, dice onion, jalapeno, and tomato. Put everything aside.

2. Shake your egg substitute, and pour it into the measuring cup. Put tomato and half of the peppers in the cup and stir. Add tobasco sauce if you want, and add salt and pepper too. Set it aside.

3. Put sausage and potatoes on the grill for five minutes. Then, add peppers and onions to the mix. After that, add your egg mixture.

4. By now grill should be at operating temperature. Place diced potatoes and sausage links on grill. After about 5 minutes, add diced peppers and onions to potatoes; mix with diced potatoes. Add egg product mixture to grill. Once

sausage is done (about 6 minutes or so,) take them out. About ten minutes, the potatoes should be done, along with the omelet. Add potatoes and links to the omelet and serve.

Waffle Panini

Enough said. Best of all, this recipe has just 470 calories.

What You Need

- 4 lightly toasted frozen waffles, preferably whole grain.
- 2 lightly beaten large eggs
- 2 tbsp of butter, divided.
- 2 slices of cheese, preferably cheddar
- 2 cooked turkey sausage patties

Direction

1. Melt one tbsp. of butter and spread it in your skillet over medium-low heat.

2. Add eggs and cook for about four minutes, not stirring. Lower heat and cook for four minutes, covered. Removing from the heat and cut in half, topping each side with cheese.

3. Put egg, cheese, and sausage on two waffles, and then top with two waffles. Put it in your press over medium heat and put one tbsp. butter in the grill.

4. Cook for four minutes, turning once until waffle is golden brown and the cheese is melted.

Breakfast Burrito

What You Need

- 1 seeded and diced jalapeno
- 1 minced garlic clove
- 1 tbsp of fresh lime juice
- ½ tsp of salt, adjust to taste
- 2 pitted, peeled, and halved large avocadoes
- 2 tbs of fresh chopped cilantro
- 3 tbsp of olive oil. Add more for brushing
- 1 seeded and diced red bell pepper
- 1 seeded and diced green bell pepper
- ¾ lb of Yukon Gold potatoes, boiled and tendered, then diced
- Black pepper to taste
- 6 bacon slices
- 12 eggs
- 6 flour tortillas
- 6 oz grated cheddar cheese
- Sour cream and salsa to serve

Directions

1. Combine jalapeno, garlic, lime juice, and salt in a small bowl. Crush with a fork until you have a coarse paste.

2. Mix in the avocados and cilantro and mash into a lumpy paste. Set your guacamole aside.

3. In a nonstick frying pan over medium heat, add 2 tbsp of olive oil. Put in the bell peppers and fry, stirring on occasion for about 8-10 minutes.

4. Put in the potatoes and cook until warmed, which should be about 3-5 minutes.

5. Add salt and pepper and keep them warm.

6. Preheat your press on the panini setting.

7. Put the bacon in the press and close your lid. Cook until crispy, which should be about 4 minutes.

8. Drain grease on paper towels, and wipe off your press.

9. In another bowl, beat eggs, salt, and pepper.

10. In a frying pan over medium-high, warm 1 tbsp of olive oil.

11. Add your eggs and stir occasionally. Do it for 2-3 minutes or until curds appear.

12. Put a spoonful of the eggs in the center of your tortilla, and top with bell peppers and one crumbled bacon slice, as well as an ounce of cheese.

13. Roll it into a burrito and brush the outside with olive oil.

14. Put two burritos in your press and close the lid.

15. Cook for about 2-3 minutes, or until crispy.

16. Repeat for the remaining burritos.

17. Serve with salsa, sour cream, and guacamole.

Chapter 3 – Time for Lunch!

Lunch is considered by many to be the middle meal of the day, a sort of appetizer until dinner. However, that doesn't mean that you have to settle for less. With your panini press, you can make many delicious dishes that can be whipped up in minutes. After all, this is a griddle known for making sandwiches, but there are so many foods you can cook in addition to that. So why settle for less? This chapter will cover all the lunch classics, from chicken, burgers, and even the classic grilled cheese. With that, here are the recipes.

Chicken

This simple grilled recipe is low in calories and fat, but high in protein and taste!

What You Need

- 2 boneless and skinless chicken breasts, about ½" in thickness
- 1 tbsp of olive oil
- ½ tsp salt
- ½ tsp of black pepper
- ½ tap of paprika
- ½ tsp of parsley flakes

Directions:

1. Preheat press for about five minutes using the high setting.

2. Coat both sides of your chicken breasts with olive oil.

3. Mix paprika, parsley, and salt on a plate, and cover both sides with chicker generously. Poke chicken with a fork a few times.

4. Put meat into heated grill and grill for about five minutes, closing the lid.

5. After that, rotate meat about ¼ of a turn and cook for a couple more minutes. Make sure there is no pink in the middle.

6. Serve.

Homemade Pizza

This rustic-looking pizza is great for a quick lunch. And you can cook it on your grill.

What You Need

- Olive oil, for brushing
- Aluminum foil
- 1 lb of fresh pizza dough
- Pesto sauce
- Cheese, pepperoni, and whatever toppings you want.

Directions

1. Set your press to high and make sure it's flat.

2. Brush olive oil on foil in a 6-inch circle. Or, just use cooking spray.

3. Divide dough into 6 servings. Stretch dough into a circle.

4. Do it as thin as possible for easy cooking.

5. Add your sauce to the pizzas.

6. Top with cheese and add whatever ingredients you want to it.

7. lace on pizza, and adjust the lid so it's barely hovering over the pizza.

8. Cook for about 6-8 minutes, and then serve.

Burgers

This recipe is a classic, and you can make great hamburgers using your panini press.
What You Need

- Ground Beef, around 80-85% lean
- Seasonings, to taste

Directions

1. Heat press on a medium high setting.

2. Season your beef with whatever you want, and then form into patties.

3. Make sure they have about the same size and thickness.

4. Put burgers on grill and close the lid.

5. Cook for about 6-8 minutes, and then add them to your buns.

6. Top with whatever you like.

7. Make sure to scrape the grill afterwards.

8. If you want to grill your buns, put them in for about a couple minutes.

Turkey Quesadilla

This recipe is cheesy and delicious! With your panini press, you can make it in no time at all too!

What You Need

- 1 flour tortilla
- 2 slices of deli turkey
- 1 handful of shredded cheese
- Add other ingredients to your liking, such as veggies if you wish.

Directions

1. Preheat on medium high, and while it's heating, sprinkle half of your cheese on one half of the tortilla.

2. Add turkey to the top of shredded cheese, and put the remaining cheese on top of your turkey.

3. Add any other ingredients that you wish.

4. Once that's done, fold your tortilla in half.

5. Put it in your press and close the lid.

6. Cook for about a minute, or until everything's melted. Take off the press and serve.

Basil-Lemon Grilled Cheese

A great twist on an old recipe, this will have everyone talking.

What You Need

- 1 cup of shredded mozzarella
- 2 oz of crumbled feta
- 2 tsp grated lemon zest
- 2 tsp chopped basil, fresh
- 1 tbsp of extra-virgin olive oil
- 8 slices of Italian bread (or sourdough,) sliced from a bakery load.

Directions

1. Heat your press to medium high.

2. While it's heating, toss your cheeses, lemon, and basil in a medium bowl.

3. Brush olive oil on two slices of your bread to give the outside some flavor.

4. Flip over a slice and top with cheese mix. Close the sandwich with your other bread slice, making sure the oiled size is up.

5. Grill two panini with the lid closed for about five minutes or until bread is toasted and cheese is melted.

Chapter 4 – Dinner Time!

Dinner is considered by many to be the big meal that restores your energy after a long day. Whether you're getting home from work or slaving over a stove all day, dinner is said to be the reward at the end of the tunnel.

As such, there are five great recipes here to make dinnertime more fun. Best of all, many of these recipes can be cooked in a flash. Because of this, you don't have to worry about wasting too much time over the stove, and instead do the things you like. Whether it's for your spouse, for your kids, or for yourself, you can make a satisfying meal using your indoor grill.

Grilled Shrimp

Seafood is great on the grill, and you can make grilled shrimp that is sure to please. You can serve this with a variety of dishes, so mix and match if you want.

What You Need

- 1 lb of medium shrimp, without veins or shells
- ½ tsp of salt
- 1 tsp of black pepper
- 1 ½ tsp of paprika
- ½ tsp of garlic powder
- ½ tsp of onion powder
- Cooking spray
- Storage bag

Directions

1. Put the shrimp in the storage bag, and add the ingredients.

2. Seal the bag and shake until the shrimp is covered with the ingredients. Place in the fridge for a half hour.

3. Then, spray the grill and preheat on high. Put shrimp into the grill and cook for about five minutes, or until firm and opaque. Serve and enjoy.

Chickpea and Avocado Panini

This panini is a delicious sandwich for vegetarians and meat eaters alike, because it packs plenty of flavor.

What You Need for the Avocado and Chickpeas

- 15 oz of chickpeas, drained, peeled, and rinsed
- 1 large avocado, peeled, pitted, and quartered
- 2 tbsp of basil, chopped
- 2 tbsp of Italian parsley, chopped
- 2 tbsp of chopped scallions
- 2 tbsp of lemon juice
- Salt and black pepper to taste

What You Need for Panini

- 4 tbsp of room temperature butter
- 8 slices of Italian bread.
- 4 tbsp of basil pesto
- ¼ cup of roasted red bell peppers, sliced
- 4 oz of sliced sharp cheese, such as Asiago
- 4 tablespoons basil pesto
- 1/4 cup sliced roasted red bell peppers
- 4 ounces Asiago or other sharp cheese, sliced

Directions

1. Heat your panini press to a medium-high.

2. While it's heating, mash your chickpeas and avocado together. It can be chunky.

3. Add in the parsley, basil, scallions, and lemon juice, seasoning with salt and pepper.

4. Spread your butter on the bread slices. Then, flip them over and spread pesto on the other side.

5. Add cheese to one slice as well as the smashed chickpeas and avocados, bell peppers, and even more cheese. Close your sandwich with the other side, making sure the buttered side faces up.

6. Put them in the press with the lid closed. Grill for about five minutes, or until the bread is toasted and your cheese is melted.

Sweet Pork Chops

These pork chops are not only delicious, but can be cooked on your presser.

What You Need

- 2 center cut pork chops, around 4 oz a piece.
- ¼ cup of brown sugar
- 2 tbsp of vegetable oil
- 1 tbsp of soy sauce
- 1 tsp of honey
- 1 tbsp of cornstarch
- ¼ cup of water
- A pinch of salt and black pepper

Directions

1. Mix your vegetable oil, sugar, honey, soy sauce, and salt and pepper in a saucepan, and then bring it to a boil.

2. In another cup, mix water and cornstarch.

3. Slowly pour your well-whisked mixture into the saucepan. Set it aside.

4. Meanwhile, preheat your grill on medium-high.

5. Put the pork chops on the press, and close the lid. Grill it for about 8 minutes, and then open up the lid.

6. Brush your pork chops with your mixture. Cook for a couple more minutes, making sure that your mixture doesn't born.

7. When done, remove them from the grill and pour the mix on it.

Classy Steak

Now you don't have to go to an expensive steakhouse to get some steaks. You can make a quality cut from home, and it'll be on the same level as a $30 steak you get at a steakhouse.

What You Need

- 1 8 oz sirloin

- Some olive oil

- 1 clove of garlic

- Salt and black pepper

Directions

1. Preheat grill on medium high. While it's heating, pound your steak with a meat hammer.

2. Make sure it's about ½ inch thick. Cut six slits on each side, and fill it with garlic.

3. Use your brush and cover both sides with olive oil. Make sure you season it with some salt and pepper.

4. Put the steak in the grill. For a medium-rare steak, do it for 4-7 minutes.

5. Do it from 6-9 for medium, or more if you like yours fully cooked. Let steak cool for five minutes before you serve.

Honey and Ginger Salmon

Gotta love some delicious salmon, right? This recipe is lean and good for you. For best results, use smaller pieces so that it's easier to grill.

What You Need

- 2 fillets of salmon
- 2 tbsp of soy sauce
- 1 tsp of garlic powder
- 3 tbsp of honey
- ½ tsp of ground ginger
- ¼ cup of orange juice
- 1 green onion, chopped

Directions

1. Combine soy sauce, garlic, honey, ginger, orange juice, and onion, all in a baking dish.

2. Take out a cup to use later. Put in your fillets and marinate for about 30 minutes.

3. After it's getting close, preheat your grill on high.

4. Add your fillets and close the lid.

5. Grill for about 5-8 minutes.

6. To figure out when it's done, use your fork and see if it flakes. If it flakes with ease, it's done.

7. Put on the rest of your marinade when it's the last minute of your grilling. Serve.

Chapter 5 – Dessert!

If you believe that your press can only make meals and not dessert, you couldn't be more wrong. With a panini press or indoor grill, you can make so many delicious desserts that it will satisfy anyone's sweet tooth. From chocolate to even cakes, there's something in here for everyone.

Dessert is seen by many to be a reward. You shouldn't eat a sweet treat every day, after all. But when you have a craving, it can't be helped. This chapter will cover some that you can make, and even some healthier options involving fruit.

Nutella Chocolate Death Panini

You heard that right. Everyone's favorite spread has its own panini, and it is tasty!

What You Need:

- 8 slices of enriched bread, i.e. challah or brioche
- 8 tbsp of Nutella. Substitute another chocolate spread if you don't want Nutella
- 4 tbsp of small chocolate chips

Directions

1. Preheat your press to high.

2. While it's heating, grab two slices of bread and spread your Nutella on each of them, a tablespoon apiece.

3. Pour a tbsp. of chocolate chips and close the slices.

4. Put two slices in there at a time.

5. Close the lid. It should take about a minute.

6. Don't grill it for an excessive amount of time, or your chocolate chips could melt.

Grilled Peach Delight

Yes, you can even grill fruit on a press. This is ideal if you want a healthy dessert.

What You Need

- 6 firm and ripe large peaches
- 12 oz of fresh or frozen raspberries
- 3 tbsp water
- 1 ½ tbsp. sugar
- 8 oz of mascarpone cheese
- ¾ cup of heavy cream
- ¼ cup of sugar to taste
- 1 tsp vanilla extract

Directions

1. Preheat your grill to medium.

2. Meanwhile, cut your peaches in half, starting at top.

3. Remove the pits, and cut each half into fourths.

4. Put the peaches in the grill on their sides on the grates.

5. Grill for 3-5 minutes until they have grill marks and are tender.

6. Make sure to grill the other side.

7. Meanwhile, make a puree of sugar, water, and raspberries until it's smooth. Strain through a mesh strainer so that the seeds are gone. Press your solids so that you get lots of sauce. This sauce can be refrigerated for two days.

8. To make the whip, combine cream, vanilla, ¼ cup of sugar, and mascarpone.

9. Beat it with an electric mixer until you see firm peaks. You can refrigerate this mixture for two hours.

10. Serve a dollop with grilled peaches and a drizzle of sauce.

For the mascarpone whip:
1. In a medium bowl, combine the mascarpone, heavy cream, vanilla, and remaining 1/4 cup of sugar.

2. Beat the mascarpone mixture with an electric mixer until medium-firm peaks form. This can be made ahead and refrigerated for a few hours.

Ice Cream Cones

Yes, you can make your own ice cream cones in your press! These are delicious and beat the store-bought kind.

What You Need

- 1 cup of heavy cream
- 1 ½ tsp vanilla extract
- 1 ½ cups of powdered sugar
- 1 ½ cups of all-purpose flower
- ¼ tsp of ground cinnamon
- A pinch of ground nutmeg
- 1 tbsp of ground cornstarch
- Wax paper
- Cone mold

Directions

1. Whip your cream and vanilla until it forms a mousse.

2. In another bowl, sift your dry ingredients. Then, add them to the cream and stir until you form a batter.

3. Allow the batter to sit for a half hour.

4. Once it's close to 30 minutes, preheat your grill to medium high.

5. Add a big tablespoon of your batter onto the grill and close your lid, pressing it down.

6. Grill for a minute and a half until it's browned but still can be bent into a shape.

7. Put the pressed cone onto a piece of waxed paper.

8. Using a cone mold, position it in the center of the cone.

9. Roll your cone around the cone mold, making sure that you do it carefully, as it may be hot.

10. Leave it there for ten seconds so that it stays in shape.

11. Repeat with the rest of the batter. Put some ice cream in it and enjoy!

Donut Chips

These make a quick snack to munch on, and they're delicious.

What You Need

- 25 soft glazed donut holes.
- ¼ cup of cinnamon sugar

Directions

1. Preheat your press to medium.

2. Meanwhile, cut each hole in half and cover both sides with cinnamon sugar.

3. Put the halves cut side up on the press, in batches.

4. Close and toast for about 40 seconds.

5. Once that happens, transfer chips onto rack so they can cool. Once they're cool, enjoy.

Mini Yellow Layer Cake with Chocolate Buttercream

We've saved the best for last. This cake is small, but packs a punch. It's great for a party or serving a quick treat for anyone's sweet tooth.

What You Need for the Cake

- 1 egg

- 2 tbsp of sugar

- 2 tbsp of melted butter

- 1 tsp of vanilla extract

- ¼ cup of all-purpose flower

- ¼ big teaspoon of baking powder

- A pinch of salt

- 1 ½ tbsp. of milk

What You Need for the Buttercream

- 3 tbsp of melted unsalted butter

- 3 tbsp of cocoa

- 1 cup powdered sugar, sifted

- 1 ½ tbsp. of milk

- ¼ tsp of vanilla extract

Directions for Yellow Cake

1. Preheat the panini grill at about 350 F.

2. Make sure your grill is flat and not tilted.

3. Spray two 6 oz ramekins with baking spray.

4. Then, in a small bowl, combine the egg and sugar with a whisk.

5. Add vanilla and butter, then mix in your baking powder, flour, and salt.

6. When the batter is smooth, add the milk.

7. Divide your batter in equal parts in the ramekins, about halfway.

8. Lay your ramekins on the grill and close your lid. The upper grates should contact the ramekins' upper edges. Bake for about 17-19 minutes, or until the cake spring back when touched. Let them cool for five minutes in the ramekins and then put them on a rack and let them cool some more.

Directions on Buttercream

1. Combine butter and cocoa.

2. Then, add in the powdered sugar, vanilla, and milk, and whisk until smooth.

3. Assemble the layers and frost with chocolate buttercream. Sprinkles are optional, but sure are fun.

4. To make the chocolate buttercream:

5. In a small bowl, whisk together the butter and cocoa. Add in the powdered sugar, milk and vanilla and whisk until the frosting is smooth.

Conclusion

Now you know just how much variety you can cook when you use your grill. You can fry up some crispy bacon, make a killer burrito, grill some shrimp, and even bake your own personal cake. Indoor grilling can be inexpensive, fun, and can save you a night out in the town. If you want to learn more recipes, do your research, or ask a few friends for suggestions. There are hundreds more recipes you can make with your panini press, and this book is just a starter.

Thank you for downloading this book! If you want to learn about all the other books we have to offer, check out our Amazon page. While you're at it, leave a review and tell us what you think. Feedback is important, and gives us more suggestions when writing our next book. Whether it's positive or negative, we'll appreciate honesty.

Now that you know more about indoor grilling, the next step is to try out some of the recipes. Go out and give it your all. Cooking is something that you can get better at, so practice with these recipes, and soon you'll be the family chef who everyone loves. You don't have to have a huge backyard and a bulky grill to make delicious foods. Anyone can make these. A college kid, a person living in the apartment, and even grandpa. It's something that's easy and fun for almost everyone in your family.

HIGH PROTEIN
LOW CARB
COOKBOOK

20 Simple, Healthy and Delicious Slow Cooker Recipes for Weight Watchers

Diana Barkley

Low Carb: Low Carb Recipes.

20 Slow Cooker Recipes for Weight Watchers

Introduction

Slow cookers (or 'crock pots' as they are known in the United States) have experienced a huge revival in popularity in recent years. They have been making reappearance onto many wedding gift lists, as an essential culinary appliance, as well as people buying them for their own use. Not only are slow cookers convenient, but they also are very energy efficient, using the equivalent heat of two bright light bulbs to cook food over many hours. They have also become cheaper and cheaper to buy, as the technology to insulate and heat them has improved.

Slow cookers are designed to be left on for long periods, and it is perfectly safe to leave them in operation while you are out of the house or overnight. Many come with a digital timer included, so you can add the raw ingredients to the slow cooker, then set it to come on at a later time, meaning that the food will be perfectly cooked by the time you get home from work. (It is not a good idea, however, to leave food without refrigeration for long periods, so do not set them up too far in advance.)

Cheaper cuts of meat work best in a slow cooker — you are looking for something that requires long cooking, such as braising steak or chicken thighs, to tenderize it. Trim off any excess fat from the meat, since this will not drain away or caramelize as it would on a roasted joint, and it is usually preferable to take off skin from the meat — slow cookers will not provide you with crispy outsides or crunchy crackling.

When buying a slow cooker, think about how large you need it to be. The smaller and medium models will heat up faster and have a more even temperature distribution, but remember that you should not fill a slow cooker to the brim. So a model with a stated capacity of five liters will be able to cook around four liters of food (check the manufacturer's instructions as to the optimum capacity for particular models.) Also, a glass lid is a useful additional feature — since you should try to avoid removing the lid as much as possible during cooking, this allows you to check on the progress of your food. Some also cook the food inside a removable pot which is attractive enough to take straight to the table, thus saving on washing up.

Some people find that the appearance of slow cooked food is unattractive, since meat and vegetables can appear 'pallid'. This is because the meat does not brown — the conditions inside the pot are not hot or dry enough to caramelize the sugars in the meat (the so-called Maillard Reaction). It is best to brown the meat before cooking — some slow cookers have an additional function for you to brown meat without having to use a separate pan.

Another thing to remember is that the pot is sealed, so that liquid will not evaporate. This also means that the sauce will not naturally thicken, so you may like to add some flour or cornflour to stop it becoming too watery. Or, if you are entirely gluten free, you can remove the meat and blend the vegetables to make a thicker gravy.

It is also possible to cook rice and pasta in a slow cooker, although since the cooking times for these will be shorter, it is best to add them towards the end of the cooking time. Rice needs to be washed very thoroughly before adding to the slow cooker, or the starchy may cause it to become claggy.

Unless specifically stated on the manufacturer's instructions, you should avoid putting the slow cooker pot in the fridge. If you want to prepare ingredients the night before, these should be put into a separate tub for refrigeration. This is because a cold pot will take a longer time to heat up, and may affect cooking times and hence food safety. For similar reasons, you should never add frozen meat or vegetables directly to the slow cooker, or use it to defrost anything that is already frozen.

Chapter 1 – Jerk Chicken

For the Jerk Sauce:

8 spring onions, chopped roughly into chunks
3 tablespoons of vegetable or olive oil
2 chilies, stemmed and seeded (adjust the heat of the final dish by choosing hotter or milder chilies or by leaving the seeds in)
1 piece of fresh ginger, peeled and sliced — start with a piece the size of your thumb
2 tablespoons of molasses or treacle
3 garlic cloves, peeled
1 tablespoon fresh thyme, or 1 teaspoon dried
2 teaspoons allspice
1/4 teaspoon ground cardamom
A big pinch of salt
For the dish:
12 to 14 skin-on chicken pieces such as thighs, legs, and split breasts
lime wedges (optional, to serve)

Method:

Combine all sauce ingredients in a food processor and pulse to a fine paste. Save a generous tablespoon of the mixture in the fridge, then pour the rest into your slow cooker and add the chicken pieces. Stir until they are coated thoroughly and cook on low for around four to six hours.

When the chicken is tender, remove from the slow cooker and transfer to a wire rack over a baking tray. You may want to put a piece of kitchen foil below to catch any sauce and make it easier to clean up afterwards. Brush the chicken with a little of the reserved paste and grill under a high heat for five minutes until browned and crispy, turning halfway through (you may need to do this in batches). Serve with lime wedges.

Chapter 2 – Vegetable Frittata

Although most people associated slow cookers with stews and casseroles, the low heat is also perfect of cooking this delicious frittata. Set your slow cooker going, then head out for a Sunday morning walk and return to a tasty, healthy brunch.

You will need:

Leafy vegetable such as kale or cooked spinach — do not use raw spinach as it will create too much water.
Two roasted red peppers diced into bite sized pieces.
Five sliced spring onions.
4-5 oz. crumbled Feta, halloumi or goat's cheese.
Eight eggs.
Salt and pepper
Sour cream for serving (optional)

Method:

Add the vegetables to the slow cooker and spread out into an even, flat layer. Beat the eggs with a good pinch of salt and pepper (you can also add other seasonings if you like, such as herbs, chili or paprika) and pour over the vegetables. Crumble over the cheese and set your slow cooker on low for two hours. Serve cut into squares with sour cream.

Tip:

This frittata is just as good hot as cold and will keep in the fridge for several days.

Chapter 3 – Lamb Shanks and Beans

<u>You will need:</u>

4 lamb shanks

1 can cannellini/white beans, rinsed and drained

6 diced peeled carrot

2 chopped onion

4 stalks of chopped celery

2 garlic cloves, chopped

2 teaspoons dried tarragon

Large pinch of salt and pepper

1 can chopped tomatoes

Method:

Add the beans, carrots, onions and celery to the slow cooker and spread out in an even layer over the base of the slow cooker. Trim any excess fat from lamb shanks and place on top of the vegetables. Sprinkle with the tarragon, salt, and pepper and add the tomatoes.

Cook on high for one hour, then reduce to low and simmer for eight to nine hours.

When the lamb is cooked, remove it from the cooker and allow it to relax. Pour the vegetables and beans through a sieve, reserving the liquid. Allow the liquid to stand while you shred the meat from the bones — it should come away very easily with a fork, leaving the bones entirely clean. Skim any fat which has risen to the surface of the liquid, then recombine the lamb, vegetables and sauce and serve.

Chapter 4 – Asian Style Beef

You will need:

3 lbs of braising beef
Four tablespoons of soy sauce
Two tablespoons of rice wine vinegar
Two tablespoons of brown sugar
Two tablespoons of ketchup
Two tablespoons of sesame seeds
1 inch of ginger grated
chili sauce to taste — depending on how hot you like it
8 whole cloves of garlic
One red onion, finely chopped
Fresh red chillies (optional, again, to personal taste)

Method:

Trim any fat from the beef, and brown it, if you wish. Mix the soy sauce, vinegar, brown sugar, ketchup, sesame seeds, ginger, and chilli sauce.

Put the beef into the slow cooker, add the onion, chillies and garlic, then pour over the sauce mixture. Stir to make sure everything is thoroughly coated.

Cook on low for eight hours. Shred the beef using two forks and allow the curry to stand for half an hour before serving.

Chapter 5 – French Onion Soup

This is perfect to make a large batch and freeze into portions to take to work as a delicious, low-carb lunch. It is traditionally serves with large cheese topped croutons, however, these can be omitted.

You will need:

Four white onions finely sliced into half moons
Two tablespoons of butter
One tablespoon of Worcestershire sauce
One tablespoon of balsamic vinegar
Three chopped garlic cloves
2 teaspoons of brown sugar
Good pinch of salt and pepper
3 tablespoons of plain flour
One and a half litres of vegetable or chicken stock
Two tablespoons of fresh thyme or one teaspoon of dried

Method:

Put the onions, butter, Worcestershire sauce, vinegar, garlic, brown sugar, salt, and pepper into the slow cooker for one hour on the highest setting until the onions start to brown. Stir occasionally.

Five minutes before the end of the cooking time, add the flour stir to make sure it is thoroughly mixed in.

Add the stock and thyme. Cook on low for six to eight hours.

Chapter 6 – Vegetarian Bolognaise

Not all slow cooker recipes have to include meat — it is also an ideal way to get bags of flavour from vegetable dishes. This bolognaise freezes very well, so make a big batch and portion it up. (Tip — make sure you label the tubs clearly so that it does not become confused with a dish that contains meat.)

You will need:

Two large aubergines, chopped
One diced onion
Six chopped garlic cloves
Large pinch of salt and pepper
200ml of chicken broth
Two cans of whole plum tomatoes
Two tablespoons of grated Parmesan cheese
One or two bay leaves

Method:

Add all ingredients to the slow cooker and cook on low for six to eight hours. The aubergine should completely break down, giving you a smooth sauce. For a vegan dish, make sure to omit the parmesan cheese.

Chapter 7 – Poached Salmon

This is an idea dish for entertaining — just set the salmon going and you can relax before your guests arrive.

You will need:

200ml of dry white wine
One lemon, thinly sliced
One shallot, thinly sliced
One bay leaf
Fresh herbs to taste — you may prefer tarragon, dill, or flat leafed parsley
One teaspoon of black peppercorns
A large pinch of salt
4-6 fillets of salmon, with the skin on
Fresh lemon wedges to serve (optional)

Method:
Pour the wine, lemon, shallots, bay leaf, herbs, peppercorns and salt in the slow cooker with 500ml of cold water and switch the cooker on to high for half an hour.

Sprinkle salt on the top of the salmon and add to the slow cooker, with the skin side down. Turn the cooker down to low and check after forty five minutes. If the fish has not yet cooked all the way through (the centre should be opaque and flaky) cook for a further fifteen minutes. Serve garnished with lemon wedges.

Chapter 8 – Buffalo Chicken

This filling would traditionally be served with salad in a flour tortilla, but you can easily serve it wrapped in a lettuce leaf and drizzled with sour cream.

You will need:

Three chicken breasts, skins removed
One stalk of celery, chopped
One diced onion
One clove of garlic
450ml of chicken stock
200ml of chili sauce — if you would prefer a milder dish, you can use ketchup instead.

To serve:

Iceberg lettuce, separated into large leaves
Five large carrots, grated
Two large celery stalks, thinly sliced
Sour cream

Method:

Add the chicken, onions, chopped celery, garlic, and stock to the slow cooker, and cook on low for eight hours, or high for four.

Remove the chicken from the pot and shred using two forks. Drain the stock from the slow cooker and discard all except 200 ml. Add the shredded chicken, reserved stock and chili sauce to the cooker, and cook on high for half an hour

To serve, spoon the chicken into lettuce cups, sprinkle with carrots and celery matchsticks and drizzle with sour cream.

Chapter 9 – Spicy Roast Chicken

You will need:

One whole chicken, cut into quarters
One onion, sliced into half moons
Salt and Pepper
Two teaspoons of paprika
One teaspoon of cayenne
One teaspoon of garlic powder

Method:

Use the sliced onions to cover the bottom of the slow cooker. Mix all the spices together then rub the mixture all over the chicken. Place the spiced chicken on top of the onions in the crock pot, cover and cook on the low setting for 5-6 hours. Check that the chicken is cooked through before serving — a meat thermometer is very useful for this.

The juice from the chicken will mix with the onions and can be turned into delicious gravy — simply remove the chicken and tip the onions and juices into a food processor and whizz together. This gravy will not require flour or cornflour to thicken it, meaning the final dish is completely gluten free.

Chapter 10 – Thai Red Curry Beef

You will need:

One pound of braising beef, cut into small pieces (you can also use lean beef mince if you would prefer)
One leek, washed and sliced into rounds
Two minced garlic cloves
One teaspoon of fresh minced ginger
One tablespoon of red curry paste
One can of chopped tomatoes
Half a lime zest and juice
One tablespoon of soy sauce
200ml of coconut milk

Method:

Brown the beef in a pan and add to the slow cooker with the leek, garlic, ginger, red curry paste, tomatoes, soy sauce and lime zest. Cook on low for 4 hours until the beef is tender.

Fifteen minutes before serving, add the coconut milk and lime juice and allow to warm through.

Chapter 11 – Glazed Spare Ribs

You will need:

Short beef ribs — aim for at least three per person
One tablespoon of olive oil
One glass of red wine
100 ml of balsamic vinegar
Two cloves of garlic
A few sprigs of fresh rosemary or a scattering of dried.
Salt and pepper to taste

Method:

Trim any fat from the ribs and generously salt and pepper them. Brown the ribs in the olive oil until colored on all sides — you may need to do this in batches.

Add the ribs to the slow cooker with the other ingredients and cook on low for six hours. You may like to check on them halfway through cooking to make sure each rib is thoroughly coated in the sauce.

Serve with a green salad — the meat should be falling off the bone and still very juicy.

Chapter 12 – Classic Pot Roast

This is the first dish that everyone thinks of when you say 'slow cooker' to them. But there is a reason for that — this is the best way to cook a tougher cut of meat and the end result is meltingly soft and very tasty.

You will need:

4 pound joint of sirloin roasting beef
One large onion, cut into quarters
Three garlic cloves, chopped
Four chopped carrots
Two sticks of celery, chopped
One and half large glasses of red wine (you could use beef stock instead)
Salt and Pepper to taste

Method:

Trim any obvious fat from the joint and brown all sides in a pan. This step is optional, but does help to add flavor and richness to the finished dish.

Put the joint along with all other ingredients and cook on high for one hour, followed by around six hours on low. Check the joint halfway through cooking and turn it over so that it spends an equal amount of time in the vegetables.

The vegetables can either be eaten along with the meat, or strained out and the sauce thickened to make gravy. This pot roast is also very tasty when sliced and eaten cold and will make excellent next-day sandwiches.

Chapter 13 – Spicy Fish Stew

You will need:

Two tablespoons olive oil
Two cloves of chopped garlic
Four carrots cut into rounds
Six large tomatoes cut into quarters
One sliced pepper, green or red
Half a teaspoon of fennel seed
200ml of fish or chicken stock
One and a half pounds of firm fish — you can use cod, haddock, salmon or raw prawns.
Cut the fish into one inch cubes, check for bones and remove any skin. If using large
prawns, make sure they have been deveined.
One teaspoon of caster sugar
One teaspoon of dried basil leaves or a handful of fresh leaves
One red chili, chopped (use more for a hotter dish or remove the seeds for a milder end
result)
Salt and Pepper to taste
Parsley to serve (optional)

Method:

Add the olive oil and garlic to the slow cooker, along with the carrots, tomatoes, pepper,
fennel seed, and stock. Cook on low for eight or nine hours until the vegetables are
tender.

About twenty minutes before you want to serve, add the fish, sugar, basil, salt, and
pepper to the slow cooker and stir gently, making sure not to break the fish up. Turn the
slow cooker up to high, and cook for twenty minutes, checking that the fish flakes easily
before serving. Scatter with chopped parsley, if using, and serve.

Chapter 14 – Mediterranean Chicken

You will need:

Twelve boneless, skinless chicken thighs — remove any excess fat, sinews or veins before cooking
Two carrots, cut into rounds
Two stalks of celery, chopped
One fennel bulb, with the core removed and chopped into chunks
One large onion, sliced into thin half moons
Sixteen large green olives, stones removed. You can use stuffed or plain, whichever you prefer.
Four crushed cloves of garlic
Two bay leaves (dried or fresh)
One teaspoon of dried oregano
Salt and pepper to taste
300ml of chicken stock
One tablespoon of plain flour (optional)
The juice and zest of one lemon
Parsley to serve (optional)

Method:

Add the carrots, celery, fennel, onion, olives, garlic, bay leaves, oregano, salt and pepper to the slow cooker. Lay the chicken thighs on top — these should be skinless so there is no need to brown them first.

Add the stock and an equal quantity of cold water. Cook on low for 5 to 6 hours. Remove the bay leaves and add the lemon and parsley before serving.

If you are using the flour, remove a ladle of cooking liquid and combine it with the flour. Whisk until smooth, then pour the flour mixture back into the slow cooker and stir. Cook the chicken for a further fifteen minutes until the sauce has thickened.

Chapter 15 – Chili Con Carne

This is another classic slow cooker recipe. The long, gentle cooking really brings out the flavors from the meat and vegetables.

You will need:

Two pounds of lean steak mince or braising steak, cut into tiny pieces
One diced onion
Three chopped cloves of garlic
Two peppers, either red or green, diced and deseeded
Four diced carrots
Four stalks of celery, diced
One red chili — use more for a hotter dish or remove the seeds if you prefer a milder heat
Four cans of chopped tomatoes
A squeeze of tomato puree
The spice blend—One teaspoon each of:
chili powder
oregano
basil
cumin
salt
pepper
onion powder
cayenne
To garnish (optional)
Crispy fried bacon (around four rashers)
Two ripe avocados.

Method:

Brown the mince in a pan for a few minutes and drain off any excess fat. Add to the slow cooker with all other ingredients and cook on low for six hours.

To serve, sprinkle with the bacon and slices of ripe avocado.

Chilli Con Carne is a dish that many people pride themselves on personalising. This recipe should be your starting point — feel free to adapt and change the recipe by tweaking the spice blend, adding beer or wine, using different vegetables or adjusting the heat of the final dish to anything from imperceptibly mild to blow-your-head-off fiery. To counteract this, you may like to serve your chilli with sour cream.

Chapter 16 – Lentil and Artichoke Tagine

You will need:
A dash of Olive Oil
Three diced onions
Four cloves of garlic, minced
Two teaspoons of garam masala
One teaspoon of ground cumin
500ml water
150g of red lentils, washed
Two bay leaves
The juice of one lemon
Four cans of chopped tomatoes
A large can of artichoke hearts
Salt and pepper
Parsley to serve (optional)
Chopped spring onions to serve

Method:

Brown the onions in a pan with the olive oil, and add the spices. Stir for a few minutes to release the aromatic oils, then add to the slow cooker along with the other ingredients. It is very important that the lentils are washed thoroughly to remove any grit prior to cooking, and also that you check the packet to make sure that they do not require presoaking. Cook on low for six to eight hours.

Before serving, scatter with chopped spring onions and parsley, if using.

Chapter 17 – Pulled Pork

This dish had become very popular on both sides of the Atlantic. Now you can make your own delicious pulled pork at home.

You will need:

2 onions, thinly sliced into half moons
4 medium garlic cloves, chopped
350ml of chicken stock
1 tablespoon of dark brown sugar
1 tablespoon of chili powder
1 teaspoon of salt, plus more to taste
1/2 teaspoon of ground cumin
1/4 teaspoon of ground cinnamon
Around a 5lb boneless pork shoulder —remove any strong or netting holding it together
2 cups of barbecue sauce (optional)

Method:

Put the onions and garlic in an even layer on the bottom of the slow cooker and pour in the stock. Combine the sugar, chili powder, measured salt, cumin, and cinnamon in a small bowl, then rub the spice mixture all over the pork. Put the meat on top of the onions and garlic, then cook for eight to ten hours on a low setting. Check that the pork is tender.

Take the pork out of the slow cooker and put on a chopping board. Use a sieve to strain off the liquid from the vegetables — return the vegetables to the slow cooker and set the strained liquid aside.

Shred the meat into bite-sized pieces, using two forks. It should come apart easily. You can also use this moment to check for and remove any large pieces of fat. Return the shredded meat to the slow cooker and mix in the barbecue sauce.

When the liquid has cooled slightly, skim off any fat which has risen to the top, and pour a few splashes of the liquid onto the pork shreds to moisten them. Taste the pork, season if required and add a little more of the stick if it is too dry.

Chapter 18 – Asparagus

You can also use your slow cook for sides and vegetables — ideal if you have limited space on your cooker.

You will need:

1 pound of asparagus spears
Two cloves of crushed garlic
The juice of one lemon
A few dashes of olive oil
Salt and pepper to taste

Method:

Trim the woody ends of the asparagus spears and lay them in the bottom of your slow cooker. Pour over the rest of the ingredients and cook on low for one hour. The spears should be tender, but still with some bite to them — you may want to reduce the cooking time for smaller asparagus.

Chapter 19 – Chicken Parmesan Soup

You will need:

One litre of chicken stock
One onion, chopped
Two courgettes, chopped
Two stalks of celery, chopped
A bunch of parsley, chopped
Half a teaspoon each of thyme, sage, nutmeg and paprika
Two chicken breasts, skins removed, cut into bite sized pieces
Three heaped tablespoons of grated parmesan cheese
Salt and pepper to taste

Method:

Add all the ingredients except the chicken, nutmeg and parmesan into the slow cooker. Cook on low for four hours then add the chicken for another hour. Check that it is cooked through, then add the nutmeg and parmesan. Taste and season.

Tip:

The stock and parmesan will add salt to the dish — do not add more salt until you have tasted the final product.

Chapter 20 – Italian Style Meatloaf

Although more popular in America, a meatloaf is a great way to make cheaper cuts of meat taste delicious. Just think of it as a pork pie, but without the pastry.

You will need:

For the Meatloaf:
2 lbs extra lean beef mince
2 eggs, large
2 grated courgettes — dry them on kitchen paper or squeeze out the water
Three tablespoons of grated Parmesan cheese
A bunch of finely chopped parsley
4 garlic cloves, crushed
3 tablespoons of balsamic vinegar
1 tablespoon of dried oregano
2 tablespoons of onion powder
Salt and pepper
Cooking oil spray

For the Topping:
Two tablespoons of ketchup
A handful of grated cheese — Mozzarella is best
A scattering of chopped parsley

Method:

Combine all the meatloaf ingredients in a large bowl and mix thoroughly — it is easiest to do this with your hands.

Line the bottom of your slow cooker with a double thickness of aluminium foil, leaving some overlap at the top to make it easier to lift the meatloaf once it's ready. Spray the bottom with cooking oil.

Use your hands to shape the mixture into a meatloaf and pack it into the lined slow cooker. Cook on low for 6 hours or on high for 3 hours.

When the meatloaf is cooked, spread the ketchup over the top and sprinkle with the cheese. Cook for another few minutes until the cheese melts. Remove from the cooker sprinkle over the chopped parsley and serve cut into slices.

Chapter 21 — Jambalya

This exotic, delicious dish hails from the melting pot of New Orleans, where Spanish and French flavors combined to make this fish stew.

You will need:

Two skinless, boneless chicken breast, cut into bite-size chunks
100g smoked turkey sausage, chopped
Two handfuls of chopped greens — you can use kale, cabbage or whatever you have to hand
Two chopped peppers, red, green or yellow
2 stalks of celery, thinly sliced
1 large chopped onion
400g can of chopped tomatoes
1 tablespoon quick-cooking tapioca
4 cloves garlic, minced
1 teaspoon dried thyme
1 teaspoon dried chili
200g raw prawns
A handful of chopped parsley (optional)

Method:

Add the chicken, sausage, greens, peppers, celery, and onion to your slow cooker. Add the tomatoes, tapioca, garlic, thyme, and crushed red pepper, and stir to combine. Cook on low for 5 to 6 hours or on high for 2 1/2 to 3 hours.

Half an hour before you want to serve, turn up the heat to high (if it is not already on this setting) and stir in the raw prawns. Cook for thirty minutes — check that the prawns are thoroughly cooked (they should be pink and opaque in the middle) before serving. Sprinkle with parsley.

Conclusion

I hope you have enjoyed this guide to creating low carb meals from your slow cooker. With a little preparation, you can enjoy low-effort, delicious meals which are ready when you want to be, and are far cheaper and healthier that pre-prepared 'convenience' food. With a slow cooker, you are in charge of everything that goes into your food, and can be sure that it is healthy, nutritious and low in carbohydrates.

Slow cookers are not only good for hearty, warming stews and soups — you can use them to cook impressive meals that can be shared by friends and family for special occasions. Why spend time slaving away in the kitchen, when your slow cooker could be doing all the work while you enjoy yourself?

Made in the USA
Monee, IL
30 November 2023

47835807R00039